Starring Mark Lowry

Ol' Jonah's
Tossed Into The Ocean

To the tune of, "My Bonnie Lies Over The Ocean"

Written by Martha Bolton • Illustrated by Lyn Boyer

Zonderkidz

The Children's Group of Zondervan Publishing House

Ol' Jonah was sent on a mission
to Nineveh far from the sea.
But Nineveh's people were wicked,
so Jonah thought, "God, don't send me!"
    Not me!
    Not me!
    Send anyone else but me!
    Not me!
    Not me!
    Send somebody else but me!

NINEVEH

He boarded a ship that was docked there.
Ol' Jonah was running away.
It sailed in the other direction,
while Jonah laid snoring all day.

A nasty ol' storm started brewing.
The waves beat against that poor boat.
The sailors held on to the railing
and prayed that they'd all stay afloat!
Turn back!
Turn back!
Oh, Jonah, quit running away!
You'll see.
You'll be
better off when you obey!

The storm raged and so all the sailors
tried rowing against the strong wind.
But Jonah said he was the problem,
and so the whole crew threw him in!
   Oh, no!
   Oh, no!
   What will our poor Jonah do?
   His goose
   is cooked!
   Looks like our prophet is through!

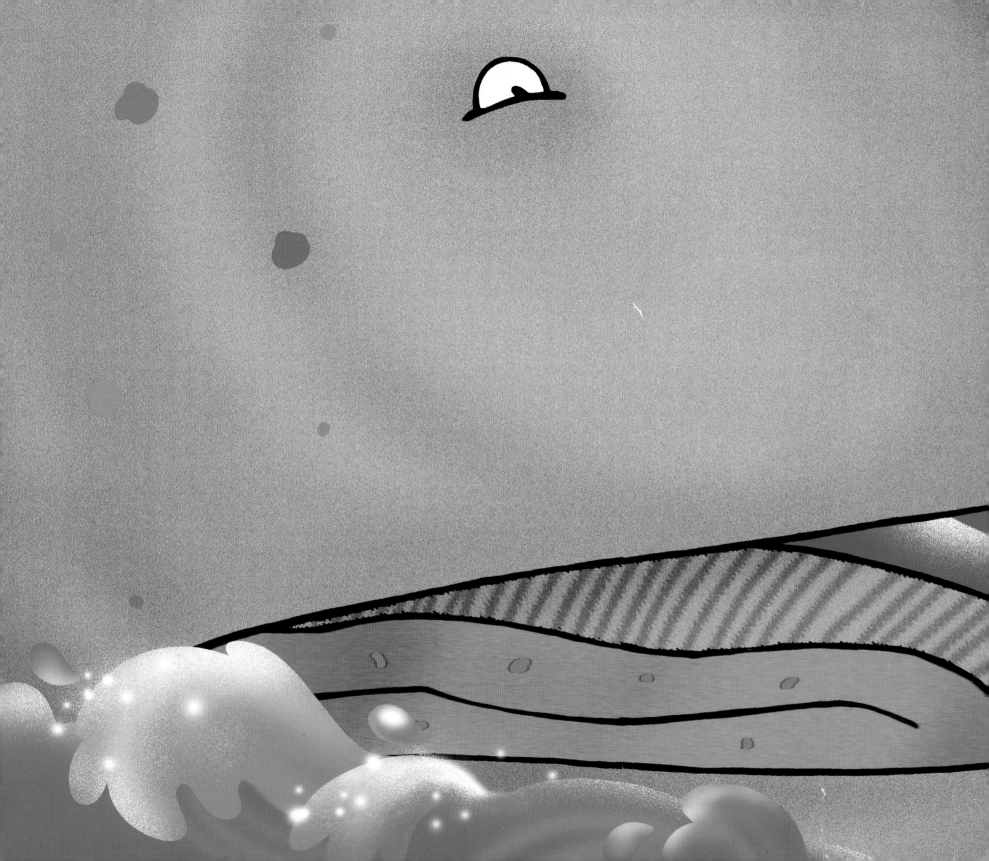

Ol' Jonah thought his life was over.
His chance for survival was slight.
But God sent a fish to the rescue,
who swallowed him up in one bite!

Then Jonah searched for a good way out.
He looked 'neath the garbage and muck.
He even crawled up in the blowhole,
but to his dismay he got stuck!

    One day,
    two days,
    a three-day vacation had he
    to think
    of where
    God wanted him to be!

Now, Nineveh started to look good,
compared to where Jonah was now.
So Jonah told God he'd obey him
if he would just free him somehow.

Stand back!

Way back!

You'd better get out of the path!

Look out!

Watch out
or you're gonna need a
good bath!

That fish started spewing out seaweed,
a wheel and a shark and a chair,
and flying out with them came Jonah,
some fifty-six feet in the air!

He landed nearby on the seashore.
He smiled just to know he was free.
The fish turned and left good ol' Jonah
and headed right back out to sea.

Then Jonah remembered his promise.
To Nineveh Ol' Jonah went.
He smiled 'cause he'd finally obeyed God,
and that fish did not charge him rent!

So, Jonah was taught a good lesson—
disobedience always brings strife.
But if we'll just learn to obey God,
He'll give us a wonderful life!
So ...

Don't fret.

Don't sweat.

Trust God and don't run away!

You'll see.

You'll be

better off when you obey!

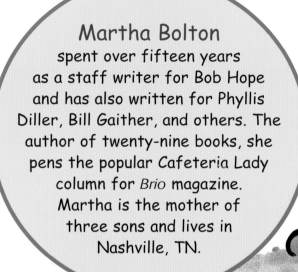

Martha Bolton
spent over fifteen years
as a staff writer for Bob Hope
and has also written for Phyllis
Diller, Bill Gaither, and others. The
author of twenty-nine books, she
pens the popular Cafeteria Lady
column for *Brio* magazine.
Martha is the mother of
three sons and lives in
Nashville, TN.

Lyn Boyer
has been an illustrator
for 20 years. Her clients
include *Reader's Digest* and
The Book of the Month Club.
Lyn and their two children
live in Williamsburg,
Michigan.

Ol' Jonah's Tossed Into The Ocean
Text copyright © 2001 by Mark Lowry and Martha Bolton
Illustrations copyright © 2001 by Lyn Boyer
Photography copyright © 2001 by Russ Harrington
Requests for information should be addressed to:

Zonderkidz™

The Children's Group of ZondervanPublishingHouse
Grand Rapids, Michigan 49530
www.zonderkidz.com

Zonderkidz is a trademark of The Zondervan Corporation.

ISBN: 0-310-70188-0

Published in association with the literary agency of Alive Communications, Inc., 7680 Goddard St., Suite 200, Colorado Springs, CO 80920.

Art direction and design by Michelle Lenger

Printed in China

01 02 03 04 05 /HK/ 10 9 8 7 6 5 4 3 2 1